© 2020 InfinitYou
All rights reserved

Get Your Free Credit Card Knive

"VALUED AT $17.95 IT'S NOW YOURS FOR FREE!"

Suitable for:
Vegetable Gardening, Outdoors, Survival, Camping, Sailing, Diving,

We're giving away these super handy Credit Card Knives for FREE! This offer will not last forever though so make sure you claim yours right now before our stock runs out!

CLAIM YOURS NOW:
harperstribune.com/knive

Annual Vegetable Garden Goals

Year

Garden Wishlist

Year

✓		✓

Garden Wishlist

Year

✓ ✓

Nurseries & Suppliers

Supplier	Name	Contact	Tel	Email	Notes

Vegetable-friendly Flowers

Flower	When to plant	Benefits, Observations and Notes

Pests and Diseases Log

Date	I.D.	Problem	Treatment	Notes

Pests and Diseases Log

Date	I.D.	Problem	Treatment	Notes

Annual Rainfall Chart

	J	F	M	A	M	J	J	A	S	O	N	D
1												
2												
3												
4												
5												
6												
7												
8												
9												
10												
11												
12												
13												
14												
15												
16												
17												
18												
19												
20												
21												
22												
23												
24												
25												
26												
27												
28												
29												
30												
31												
Total												

Seasonal Planning

Seasonal Garden Layout Planner

Months	Season

Garden Layout Notes

Month

Seasonal Planter Planner

Months	Season

Seasonal Potting Planner

Months		Season	

Plant	Date Potted	Observations and Notes

Seasonal Garden Tasks & Expenses Log

| Months | | Season | |

Item	Budget	Actual	Task	✓

Item	Budget	Actual	Notes

Notes

Month

Seasonal Garden Layout Planner

Months		Season

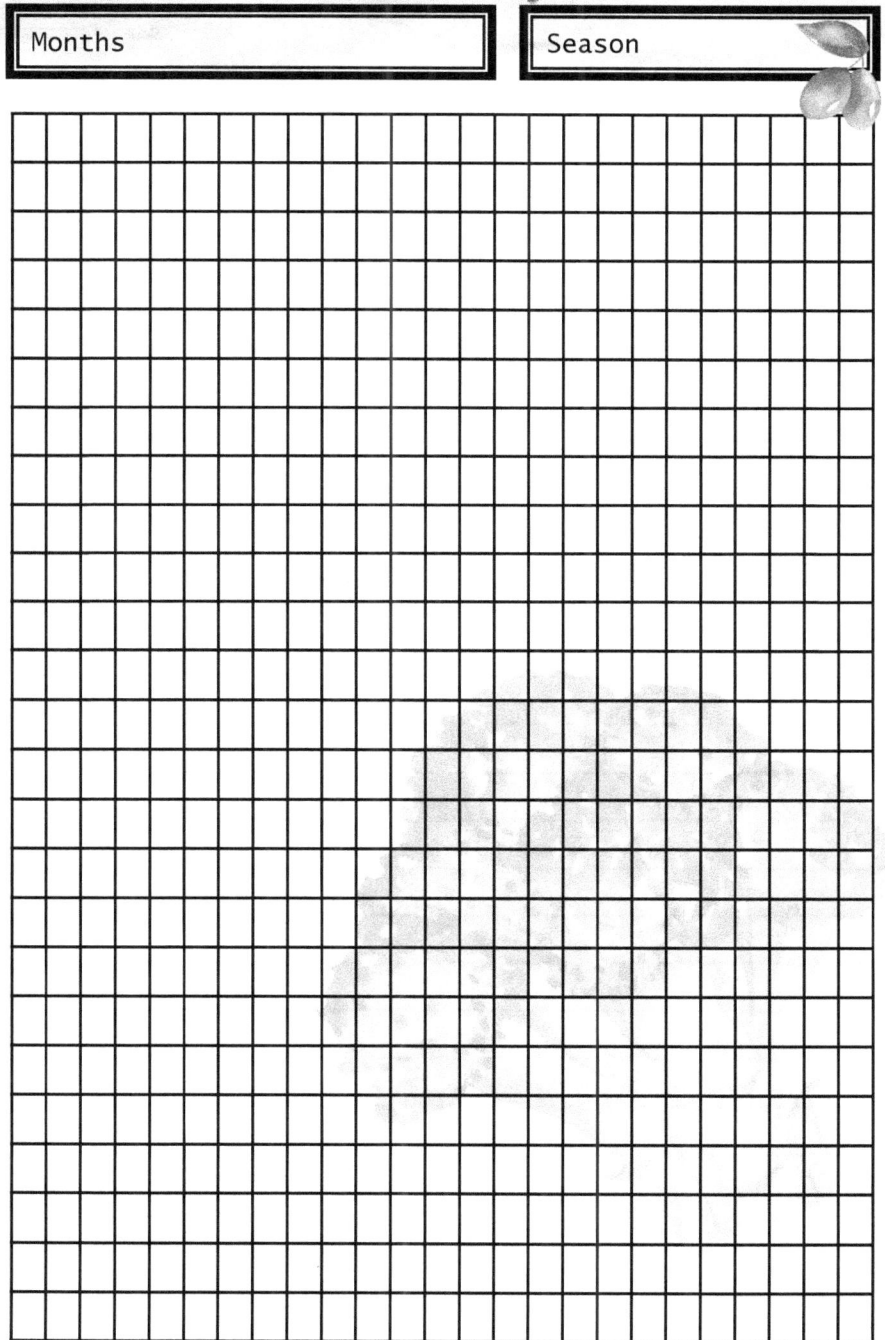

Garden Layout Notes

Month

Seasonal Planter Planner

Months	Season

Seasonal Potting Planner

Months		Season	

Plant	Date Potted	Observations and Notes

Seasonal Garden Tasks & Expenses Log

Months		Season	

Item	Budget	Actual	Task	✓

Item	Budget	Actual	Notes

Notes

Month

Seasonal Garden Layout Planner

Months	Season

Garden Layout Notes

Month

Seasonal Planter Planner

Months	Season

Seasonal Potting Planner

| Months | | Season | |

Plant	Date Potted	Observations and Notes

Seasonal Garden Tasks & Expenses Log

| Months | | Season | |

Item	Budget	Actual	Task	✓

			Notes

Notes

Month

Seasonal Garden Layout Planner

Months		Season

Garden Layout Notes

Month

Seasonal Planter Planner

Months	Season

Seasonal Potting Planner

Months		Season	

Plant	Date Potted	Observations and Notes

Seasonal Garden Tasks & Expenses Log

Months		Season	

Item	Budget	Actual	Task	✓

Item	Budget	Actual	Notes

Notes

Month

Notes

Month

Monthly Calendar

Monthly Garden Planner

Budget

Expected Weather

To Buy
- ☐
- ☐
- ☐
- ☐
- ☐
- ☐
- ☐
- ☐

Priorities
- ☐
- ☐
- ☐
- ☐
- ☐
- ☐
- ☐

Sow

Plant

Feed

Prepare

Prune

Notes

Planting Tracker

Month:

Date	Plant	Qty	Start Indoors	Transplant or Sow (T/S)	Days to Germination	Spacing	Harvest Date	Yield

Monthly Harvest Calendar

Month

Mon	Tues	Wed	Thurs	Fri	Sat	Sun
___	___	___	___	___	___	___
___	___	___	___	___	___	___
___	___	___	___	___	___	___
___	___	___	___	___	___	___
___	___	___	___	___	___	___

Notes

Progress & Notes

Month

Monthly Garden Planner

 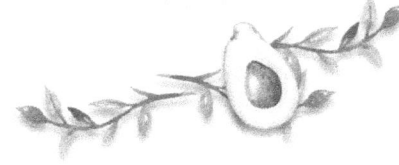

Budget

Expected Weather

To Buy
- ☐
- ☐
- ☐
- ☐
- ☐
- ☐
- ☐
- ☐

Priorities
- ☐
- ☐
- ☐
- ☐
- ☐
- ☐
- ☐
- ☐

Sow

Plant

Feed

Prepare

Prune

Notes

Planting Tracker

Month:

Date	Plant	Qty	Start Indoors	Transplant or Sow (T/S)	Days to Germination	Spacing	Harvest Date	Yield

Monthly Harvest Calendar

Month

Mon	Tues	Wed	Thurs	Fri	Sat	Sun
___	___	___	___	___	___	___
___	___	___	___	___	___	___
___	___	___	___	___	___	___
___	___	___	___	___	___	___
___	___	___	___	___	___	___

Notes

Progress & Notes

Month

Monthly Garden Planner

Budget

Expected Weather

To Buy
- ☐
- ☐
- ☐
- ☐
- ☐
- ☐
- ☐
- ☐

Priorities
- ☐
- ☐
- ☐
- ☐
- ☐
- ☐
- ☐
- ☐

Sow

Plant

Feed

Prepare

Prune

Notes

Planting Tracker

Month:

Date	Plant	Qty	Start Indoors	Transplant or Sow (T/S)	Days to Germination	Spacing	Harvest Date	Yield

Monthly Harvest Calendar

Month

Mon	Tues	Wed	Thurs	Fri	Sat	Sun

Notes

_____
_____
_____
_____
_____

Progress & Notes

Month

Monthly Garden Planner

Budget

Expected Weather

To Buy
- [ ]
- [ ]
- [ ]
- [ ]
- [ ]
- [ ]
- [ ]
- [ ]

Priorities
- [ ]
- [ ]
- [ ]
- [ ]
- [ ]
- [ ]
- [ ]
- [ ]

Sow

Plant

Feed

Prepare

Prune

Notes

Planting Tracker

Month:

Date	Plant	Qty	Start Indoors	Transplant or Sow (T/S)	Days to Germination	Spacing	Harvest Date	Yield

Monthly Harvest Calendar

Month

Mon	Tues	Wed	Thurs	Fri	Sat	Sun

Notes

Progress & Notes

Month

Monthly Garden Planner

 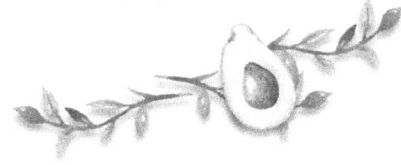

Budget

Expected Weather

To Buy
- ☐
- ☐
- ☐
- ☐
- ☐
- ☐
- ☐
- ☐

Priorities
- ☐
- ☐
- ☐
- ☐
- ☐
- ☐
- ☐
- ☐

Sow

Plant

Feed

Prepare

Prune

Notes

Planting Tracker

Month:

Date	Plant	Qty	Start Indoors	Transplant or Sow (T/S)	Days to Germination	Spacing	Harvest Date	Yield

Monthly Harvest Calendar

Month

Mon	Tues	Wed	Thurs	Fri	Sat	Sun

Notes

Progress & Notes

Month

Monthly Garden Planner

Budget	To Buy	Priorities
	☐	☐
	☐	☐
Expected Weather	☐	☐
	☐	☐
	☐	☐
	☐	☐
	☐	☐
	☐	☐

Sow	Plant	Feed	Prepare
		Prune	**Notes**

Planting Tracker

Month:

Date	Plant	Qty	Start Indoors	Transplant or Sow (T/S)	Days to Germination	Spacing	Harvest Date	Yield

Monthly Harvest Calendar

Month

Mon	Tues	Wed	Thurs	Fri	Sat	Sun
___	___	___	___	___	___	___
___	___	___	___	___	___	___
___	___	___	___	___	___	___
___	___	___	___	___	___	___
___	___	___	___	___	___	___

Notes
_____
_____
_____
_____
_____

Progress & Notes

Month

Monthly Garden Planner

Budget

Expected Weather

To Buy
- ☐
- ☐
- ☐
- ☐
- ☐
- ☐
- ☐
- ☐

Priorities
- ☐
- ☐
- ☐
- ☐
- ☐
- ☐
- ☐
- ☐

Sow

Plant

Feed

Prepare

Prune

Notes

Planting Tracker

Month:

Date	Plant	Qty	Start Indoors	Transplant or Sow (T/S)	Days to Germination	Spacing	Harvest Date	Yield

Monthly Harvest Calendar

Month

Mon	Tues	Wed	Thurs	Fri	Sat	Sun
___	___	___	___	___	___	___
___	___	___	___	___	___	___
___	___	___	___	___	___	___
___	___	___	___	___	___	___
___	___	___	___	___	___	___

Notes

Progress & Notes

Month

Monthly Garden Planner

 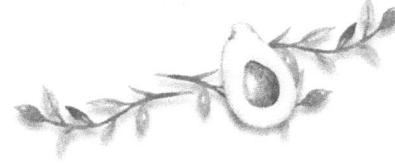

Budget

Expected Weather

To Buy
- ☐
- ☐
- ☐
- ☐
- ☐
- ☐
- ☐
- ☐

Priorities
- ☐
- ☐
- ☐
- ☐
- ☐
- ☐
- ☐
- ☐

Sow

Plant

Feed

Prepare

Prune

Notes

Planting Tracker

Month:

Date	Plant	Qty	Start Indoors	Transplant or Sow (T/S)	Days to Germination	Spacing	Harvest Date	Yield

Monthly Harvest Calendar

Month

Mon	Tues	Wed	Thurs	Fri	Sat	Sun
___	___	___	___	___	___	___
___	___	___	___	___	___	___
___	___	___	___	___	___	___
___	___	___	___	___	___	___
___	___	___	___	___	___	___

Notes
_____
_____
_____
_____
_____

Progress & Notes

Month

Monthly Garden Planner

Budget

Expected Weather

To Buy
- ☐
- ☐
- ☐
- ☐
- ☐
- ☐
- ☐
- ☐

Priorities
- ☐
- ☐
- ☐
- ☐
- ☐
- ☐
- ☐
- ☐

Sow

Plant

Feed

Prepare

Prune

Notes

Planting Tracker

Month:

Date	Plant	Qty	Start Indoors	Transplant or Sow (T/S)	Days to Germination	Spacing	Harvest Date	Yield

Monthly Harvest Calendar

Month

Mon	Tues	Wed	Thurs	Fri	Sat	Sun
___	___	___	___	___	___	___
___	___	___	___	___	___	___
___	___	___	___	___	___	___
___	___	___	___	___	___	___
___	___	___	___	___	___	___

Notes
_____
_____
_____
_____

Progress & Notes

Month

Monthly Garden Planner

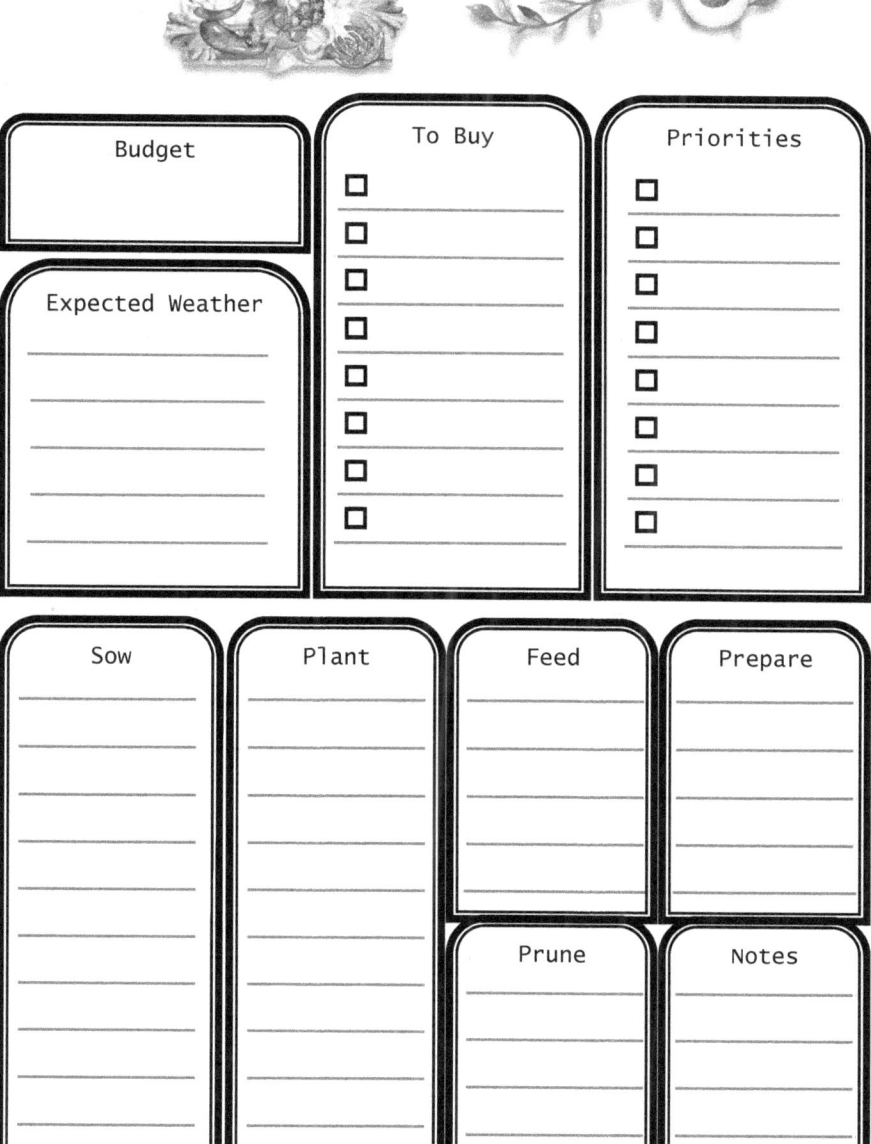

Budget	To Buy	Priorities
	☐	☐
Expected Weather	☐	☐
	☐	☐
	☐	☐
	☐	☐
	☐	☐
	☐	☐
	☐	☐

Sow	Plant	Feed	Prepare

		Prune	Notes

Planting Tracker

Month:

Date	Plant	Qty	Start Indoors	Transplant or Sow (T/S)	Days to Germination	Spacing	Harvest Date	Yield

Monthly Harvest Calendar

Month

Mon	Tues	Wed	Thurs	Fri	Sat	Sun
___	___	___	___	___	___	___
___	___	___	___	___	___	___
___	___	___	___	___	___	___
___	___	___	___	___	___	___
___	___	___	___	___	___	___

Notes
_____
_____
_____
_____
_____

Progress & Notes

Month

Monthly Garden Planner

 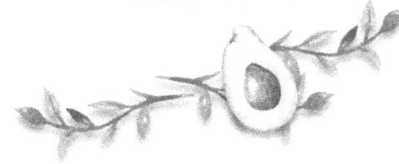

Budget

Expected Weather

To Buy
- ☐
- ☐
- ☐
- ☐
- ☐
- ☐
- ☐
- ☐

Priorities
- ☐
- ☐
- ☐
- ☐
- ☐
- ☐
- ☐
- ☐

Sow

Plant

Feed

Prepare

Prune

Notes

Planting Tracker

Month:

Date	Plant	Qty	Start Indoors	Transplant or Sow (T/S)	Days to Germination	Spacing	Harvest Date	Yield

Monthly Harvest Calendar

Month

Mon	Tues	Wed	Thurs	Fri	Sat	Sun
___	___	___	___	___	___	___
___	___	___	___	___	___	___
___	___	___	___	___	___	___
___	___	___	___	___	___	___
___	___	___	___	___	___	___

Notes

_____
_____
_____
_____
_____

Progress & Notes

Month

Monthly Garden Planner

Budget	To Buy	Priorities
	☐	☐
Expected Weather	☐	☐
	☐	☐
	☐	☐
	☐	☐
	☐	☐
	☐	☐
	☐	☐

Sow	Plant	Feed	Prepare
		Prune	**Notes**

Planting Tracker

Month:

Date	Plant	Qty	Start Indoors	Transplant or Sow (T/S)	Days to Germination	Spacing	Harvest Date	Yield

Monthly Harvest Calendar

Month

Mon	Tues	Wed	Thurs	Fri	Sat	Sun
___	___	___	___	___	___	___
___	___	___	___	___	___	___
___	___	___	___	___	___	___
___	___	___	___	___	___	___
___	___	___	___	___	___	___

Notes

Progress & Notes

Month

Progress & Notes

Month

Weekly Garden Tasks

Task	Times per Week	M	T	W	T	F	S	S	Notes

Progress & Notes

Week

Garden Notes

To Buy

Pests and Problem Areas

Weekly Garden Tasks

Task	Times per Week	M	T	W	T	F	S	S	Notes

Progress & Notes

Week

Garden Notes

To Buy

Pests and Problem Areas

Weekly Garden Tasks

Task	Times per Week	M	T	W	T	F	S	S	Notes

Progress & Notes

Week

Garden Notes

To Buy

Pests and Problem Areas

Weekly Garden Tasks

Task	Times per Week	M	T	W	T	F	S	S	Notes

Progress & Notes

Week

Garden Notes

To Buy

Pests and Problem Areas

Weekly Garden Tasks

Task	Times per Week	M	T	W	T	F	S	S	Notes

Progress & Notes

 Week

Garden Notes

To Buy

Pests and Problem Areas

Weekly Garden Tasks

Task	Times per Week	M	T	W	T	F	S	S	Notes

Progress & Notes

Week

Garden Notes

To Buy

Pests and Problem Areas

Weekly Garden Tasks

Task	Times per Week	M	T	W	T	F	S	S	Notes

Progress & Notes

Week

Garden Notes

To Buy

Pests and Problem Areas

Weekly Garden Tasks

Task	Times per Week	M	T	W	T	F	S	S	Notes

Progress & Notes

Week

Garden Notes

To Buy

Pests and Problem Areas

Weekly Garden Tasks

Task	Times per Week	M	T	W	T	F	S	S	Notes

Progress & Notes

Week

Garden Notes

To Buy

Pests and Problem Areas

Weekly Garden Tasks

Task	Times per Week	M	T	W	T	F	S	S	Notes

Progress & Notes

Week

Garden Notes

To Buy

Pests and Problem Areas

Weekly Garden Tasks

Task	Times per Week	M	T	W	T	F	S	S	Notes

Progress & Notes

Week

Garden Notes

To Buy

Pests and Problem Areas

Weekly Garden Tasks

Task	Times per Week	M	T	W	T	F	S	S	Notes

Progress & Notes

Week

Garden Notes

To Buy

Pests and Problem Areas

Weekly Garden Tasks

Task	Times per Week	M	T	W	T	F	S	S	Notes

Progress & Notes

Week

Garden Notes

To Buy

Pests and Problem Areas

Weekly Garden Tasks

Task	Times per Week	M	T	W	T	F	S	S	Notes

Progress & Notes

Week

Garden Notes

To Buy

Pests and Problem Areas

Weekly Garden Tasks

Task	Times per Week	M	T	W	T	F	S	S	Notes

Progress & Notes

Week

Garden Notes

To Buy

Pests and Problem Areas

Weekly Garden Tasks

Task	Times per Week	M	T	W	T	F	S	S	Notes

Progress & Notes

Week

Garden Notes

To Buy

Pests and Problem Areas

Weekly Garden Tasks

Task	Times per Week	M	T	W	T	F	S	S	Notes

Progress & Notes

Week

Garden Notes

To Buy

Pests and Problem Areas

Weekly Garden Tasks

Task	Times per Week	M	T	W	T	F	S	S	Notes

Progress & Notes

Week

Garden Notes

To Buy

Pests and Problem Areas

Weekly Garden Tasks

Task	Times per Week	M	T	W	T	F	S	S	Notes

Progress & Notes

Week

Garden Notes

To Buy

Pests and Problem Areas

Weekly Garden Tasks

Task	Times per Week	M	T	W	T	F	S	S	Notes

Progress & Notes

Week

Garden Notes

To Buy

Pests and Problem Areas

Weekly Garden Tasks

Task	Times per Week	M	T	W	T	F	S	S	Notes

Progress & Notes

Week

Garden Notes

To Buy

Pests and Problem Areas

Weekly Garden Tasks

Task	Times per Week	M	T	W	T	F	S	S	Notes

Progress & Notes

Week

Garden Notes

To Buy

Pests and Problem Areas

Weekly Garden Tasks

Task	Times per Week	M	T	W	T	F	S	S	Notes

Progress & Notes

Week

Garden Notes

To Buy

Pests and Problem Areas

Weekly Garden Tasks

Task	Times per Week	M	T	W	T	F	S	S	Notes

Progress & Notes

Week

Garden Notes

To Buy

Pests and Problem Areas

Weekly Garden Tasks

Task	Times per Week	M	T	W	T	F	S	S	Notes

Progress & Notes

Week

Garden Notes

To Buy

Pests and Problem Areas

Weekly Garden Tasks

Task	Times per Week	M	T	W	T	F	S	S	Notes

Progress & Notes

Week

Garden Notes

To Buy

Pests and Problem Areas

Weekly Garden Tasks

Task	Times per Week	M	T	W	T	F	S	S	Notes

Progress & Notes

Week

Garden Notes

To Buy

Pests and Problem Areas

Weekly Garden Tasks

Task	Times per Week	M	T	W	T	F	S	S	Notes

Progress & Notes

Week

Garden Notes

To Buy

Pests and Problem Areas

Weekly Garden Tasks

Task	Times per Week	M	T	W	T	F	S	S	Notes

Progress & Notes

Week

Garden Notes

To Buy

Pests and Problem Areas

Weekly Garden Tasks

Task	Times per Week	M	T	W	T	F	S	S	Notes

Progress & Notes

Week

Garden Notes

To Buy

Pests and Problem Areas

Weekly Garden Tasks

Task	Times per Week	M	T	W	T	F	S	S	Notes

Progress & Notes

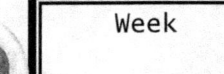
Week

Garden Notes

To Buy

Pests and Problem Areas

Weekly Garden Tasks

Task	Times per Week	M	T	W	T	F	S	S	Notes

Progress & Notes

Week

Garden Notes

To Buy

Pests and Problem Areas

Weekly Garden Tasks

Task	Times per Week	M	T	W	T	F	S	S	Notes

Progress & Notes

Week

Garden Notes

To Buy

Pests and Problem Areas

Weekly Garden Tasks

Task	Times per Week	M	T	W	T	F	S	S	Notes

Progress & Notes

Week

Garden Notes

To Buy

Pests and Problem Areas

Weekly Garden Tasks

Task	Times per Week	M	T	W	T	F	S	S	Notes

Progress & Notes

Week

Garden Notes

To Buy

Pests and Problem Areas

Weekly Garden Tasks

Task	Times per Week	M	T	W	T	F	S	S	Notes

Progress & Notes

Week

Garden Notes

To Buy

Pests and Problem Areas

Weekly Garden Tasks

Task	Times per Week	M	T	W	T	F	S	S	Notes

Progress & Notes

Week

Garden Notes

To Buy

Pests and Problem Areas

Weekly Garden Tasks

Task	Times per Week	M	T	W	T	F	S	S	Notes

Progress & Notes

Week

Garden Notes

To Buy

Pests and Problem Areas

Weekly Garden Tasks

Task	Times per Week	M	T	W	T	F	S	S	Notes

Progress & Notes

Week

Garden Notes

To Buy

Pests and Problem Areas

Weekly Garden Tasks

Task	Times per Week	M	T	W	T	F	S	S	Notes

Progress & Notes

Week

Garden Notes

To Buy

Pests and Problem Areas

Weekly Garden Tasks

Task	Times per Week	M	T	W	T	F	S	S	Notes

Progress & Notes

Week

Garden Notes

To Buy

Pests and Problem Areas

Weekly Garden Tasks

Task	Times per Week	M	T	W	T	F	S	S	Notes

Progress & Notes

Week

Garden Notes

To Buy

Pests and Problem Areas

Weekly Garden Tasks

Task	Times per Week	M	T	W	T	F	S	S	Notes

Progress & Notes

Week

Garden Notes

To Buy

Pests and Problem Areas

Weekly Garden Tasks

Task	Times per Week	M	T	W	T	F	S	S	Notes

Progress & Notes

Week

Garden Notes

To Buy

Pests and Problem Areas

Weekly Garden Tasks

Task	Times per Week	M	T	W	T	F	S	S	Notes

Progress & Notes

Week

Garden Notes

To Buy

Pests and Problem Areas

Weekly Garden Tasks

Task	Times per Week	M	T	W	T	F	S	S	Notes

Progress & Notes

Week

Garden Notes

To Buy

Pests and Problem Areas

Weekly Garden Tasks

Task	Times per Week	M	T	W	T	F	S	S	Notes

Progress & Notes

Week

Garden Notes

To Buy

Pests and Problem Areas

Weekly Garden Tasks

Task	Times per Week	M	T	W	T	F	S	S	Notes

Progress & Notes

Week

Garden Notes

To Buy

Pests and Problem Areas

Weekly Garden Tasks

Task	Times per Week	M	T	W	T	F	S	S	Notes

Progress & Notes

Week

Garden Notes

To Buy

Pests and Problem Areas

Weekly Garden Tasks

Task	Times per Week	M	T	W	T	F	S	S	Notes

Progress & Notes

Week

Garden Notes

To Buy

Pests and Problem Areas

Weekly Garden Tasks

Task	Times per Week	M	T	W	T	F	S	S	Notes

Progress & Notes

Week

Garden Notes

To Buy

Pests and Problem Areas

Weekly Garden Tasks

Task	Times per Week	M	T	W	T	F	S	S	Notes

Progress & Notes

Week

Garden Notes

To Buy

Pests and Problem Areas

Weekly Garden Tasks

Task	Times per Week	M	T	W	T	F	S	S	Notes

Progress & Notes

Week

Garden Notes

To Buy

Pests and Problem Areas

Weekly Garden Tasks

Task	Times per Week	M	T	W	T	F	S	S	Notes

Progress & Notes

Week

Garden Notes

To Buy

Pests and Problem Areas

Weekly Garden Tasks

Task	Times per Week	M	T	W	T	F	S	S	Notes

Progress & Notes

Week

Garden Notes

To Buy

Pests and Problem Areas

Weekly Garden Tasks

Task	Times per Week	M	T	W	T	F	S	S	Notes

Progress & Notes

Week

Garden Notes

To Buy

Pests and Problem Areas

Weekly Garden Tasks

Task	Times per Week	M	T	W	T	F	S	S	Notes

Progress & Notes

Week

Garden Notes

To Buy

Pests and Problem Areas

Weekly Garden Tasks

Task	Times per Week	M	T	W	T	F	S	S	Notes

Progress & Notes

Week

Garden Notes

To Buy

Pests and Problem Areas

Weekly Garden Tasks

Task	Times per Week	M	T	W	T	F	S	S	Notes

Progress & Notes

Week

Garden Notes

To Buy

Pests and Problem Areas

Weekly Garden Tasks

Task	Times per Week	M	T	W	T	F	S	S	Notes

Progress & Notes

Week

Garden Notes

To Buy

Pests and Problem Areas

Progress & Notes

Week

Garden Notes

To Buy

Pests and Problem Areas

Profile Sheets & Recipes

Profile Sheet

Name	V	H
Basil		✓

About

Popular varieties include Genovese (the most popular, used in Italian dishes), lemon, lime, purple, and Thai. (more common in Asian-influenced recipes).

Advice for Growing

An annual that is easy to grow from seed and benefits from frequent harvesting.

When plants reach 10-12" high, encourage bush form by pinching leaves from the top down to just above the second set of leaves.

Plant in full sun. Provide afternoon shade in warmer regions.

Plant in rich, well-drained soil. Water frequently, but ensure good drainage.

Notes

Use and Storage

Best when used fresh from the garden. Delicious in fresh salad or as caprese salad with fresh tomatoes and mozzarella cheese.

For larger harvests, trim ends of stems and place in a glass of water like fresh flowers. Place in direct sunlight.

Don't store cut leaves in the refrigerator.

Add fresh basil to cooked dishes when you are almost done cooking as they lose flavour and color when cooked.

Make Basil pesto by combining with olive oil, toasted pine nuts, garlic cloves and Parmesan cheese in a food processor. Add to ice cube trays and top with a little extra olive oil. Freeze and use 1-2 cubes to soups, stews and slow cooker meals.

Profile Sheet

Name	V	H
Chamomile		✓

About

Known for its medicinal qualities, primarily
for its calming, healing and soothing properties.

Roman (aka English) chamomile is a perennial creeping ground cover with daisy-like
flowers.

German chamomile is a re-seeding annual and grows upright to approx. 2fft. Both varieties are similar in terms of their use.

Advice for Growing

Easy to grow from seed, cuttings or by dividing established plants.

This plant enjoys partial shade over full sun, and prefers dry soil, making it drought tolerant.

It is a good companion plant, being a natural deterrent to many pests. Plants weakened by lack of water are more susceptible to pests, however.

Use and Storage

Commonly used to make herbal tea, essential oils and tinctures.

Chamomile tea can be made with either fresh or dried flowers. For best results, harvest chamomile flowers when the plant is totally dry.

To harvest, pluck the individual flower heads from the plants or cut full stems.

Allow individual flowers to dry completely on a baking sheet or some cheesecloth. Hang stems upside down in an area with good air circulation.

Once dry, remove the flower petals and discard the leaves and stems before using. Store in an airtight container away from sunlight.

NOTE: Check with your medical practitioner before using Chamomile for medicinal purposes.

Notes

Profile Sheet

Name	V	H
Chives		✓

About

Grown for their leaves and the beautiful, edible purple flowers they yield each spring. Both the leaves and flowers have a delicate oniony flavour.

These are hardy perennials that prefer full sun, but they can also tolerate partial shade.

If possible, provide some afternoon shade in warmer climates.

Advice for Growing

These are hardy perennials and prefer full sun. If possible, provide some afternoon shade in warmer climates.

For best results, plant chives in well-drained soil rich in organic material.

Ensure good drainage for best performance. Chives are ideal for container and raised bed gardens. Make sure your plants receive plenty of water until they are well established and during the growing season..

After 3 – 4 years divide clumps during the spring.

Notes

Use and Storage

Commonly used to make herbal tea, essential oils and tinctures.

Chamomile tea can be made with either fresh or dried flowers. For best results, harvest chamomile flowers when the plant is totally dry.

To harvest, pluck the individual flower heads from the plants or cut full stems.

Allow individual flowers to dry completely on a baking sheet or some cheesecloth. Hang stems upside down in an area with good air circulation.

Once dry, remove the flower petals and discard the leaves and stems before using. Store in an airtight container away from sunlight.

NOTE: Check with your medical practitioner before using Chamomile for medicinal purposes.

Profile Sheet

Name	V	H
Cilantro		✓

About

The flat parsley-like leaves give a distinctive flavor to guacamole, salsa and other Mexican recipes. The seeds (Coriander seeds) are ground into a powder or used whole in many popular Indian dishes.

Advice for Growing

This is a very fast grower and easy to grow from seed, taking only 3-4 weeks from the time the seeds are planted before it can be harvested.

This herb prefers full sun, with a little afternoon shade in hot regions. It also performs best in well-drained, moist soil. Raised beds or containers are ideal locations as long as they receive adequate water.

To extend harvests throughout the growing season, keep reseeding every 2 or 3 weeks to ensure a steady supply of fresh leaves.

Notes

Use and Storage

To harvest, cut the leafy stems almost to ground level. Leave 2/3 of the plant intact and allow it to regenerate before harvesting again.

Best added right at the end of cooking or in cold dishes like salsa or guacamole.

Best enjoyed fresh, but it doesn't last long once cut. Keep cut stems placed in a jar filled with water in the refrigerator with a plastic bag placed loosely over the top of the leaves.

To freeze, wash, dry and chop cilantro and toss with some olive oil. Spoon into ice cube trays and freeze. Use cubes for salsa, guacamole or other recipes. Drying is not recommended as leaves lose their flavour when dried.

Profile Sheet

Name	V	H
Dill		✓

About

A versatile culinary herb where almost all parts of the plant, including its leaves, flowers, stems and seeds, can be used.

This self-seeding biennial provides beauty in the garden with its wispy leaves and delicate
yellow flowers.

Advice for Growing

Performs best in more moderate climates and does not do well in extreme hot or cold weather. Choose a sunny, well-drained spot with rich soil.

The regular dill plant reaches 2-4 ft in height, the more diminutive Fearnleaf variety usually only grows to approx. 18". Make sure you select the correct variety for your planting area.

Notes

Use and Storage

Fresh from the garden is best and most versatile. The feathery leaves have the least intense flavor and can be snipped off the plant as needed for salads, dressings or marinades. This herb is delicious garnish and goes well with fish.

Dill seeds have the most flavor and can be used whole or ground into a powder. Use them for a pickling spice or try them with colorful vegetables. The seeds also go well in homemade bread.

Add the yellow flowers to pickle jars or toss in salads for a color and flavor. Save stems to make broth.

Preserve in olive oil, vinegar, butter or by freezing in water or oil.

Profile Sheet

Name	V	H
Echinacea		✓

About

It is believed that Native Americans used Echinacea to treat illness for hundreds of years before the arrival of the European settlers. Echinacea is used to improve immune function and reduce the severity of many ailments, including the common cold, flu and upper respiratory infections.

Advice for Growing

Echinacea is also popular for its ornamental blooms. The most common variety of Echinacea is known as purple coneflower, because of its bright petal color. Blooms are also found in many other colors.

This is an easy-to-grow perennial and can be grown from seed, transplants or by division. It is a very hardy plant that can thrive in

most conditions with very little attention. Although it prefers full sun, it will do well in light shade. In hot climates, shade yields more vibrantly colored flowers.

Notes

Use and Storage

Use the petals, leaves and roots of Echinacea to make herbal tea or tinctures.

Harvest the leaves and flowers as soon as the flowers begin to bloom by snipping each stem right above the bottom set of leaves. Remove the flower buds and leaves and discard the stems. Allow to dry thoroughly in an interior room. Exposure to sunlight can reduce the efficacy of Echinacea after cutting and remaining moisture can lead to mold.

Harvest roots in the fall after the foliage has turned brown. Hand dig some, but leave plenty for next year's growth. Wash thoroughly and allow to dry for several days on screens.

Store dried petals, leaves and roots in an airtight container in a pantry or cupboard until ready to use.

Check with your medical practitioner before using herbs for medicinal purposes.

Profile Sheet

Name	V	H
Fennel		✓

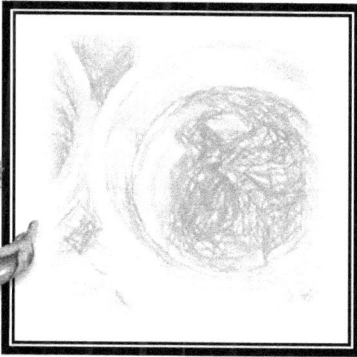

About

There are two main types of fennel - Herb fennel and the white bulb-type vegetable. This page focuses on the herb type.

Common sweet fennel resembles dill with its wispy foliage. Other varieties of herb fennel are more popular for their bronze or red leaves. In mid-to-late summer, fennel produces delicate yellow flowers.

Advice for Growing

Fennel is short-lived, but will reseed naturally. Plants reach 3- 5 feet high so provide ample room for growth, depending on the
varieties you are growing.

This herb prefers full sun and rich, well-drained soil. It is drought tolerant, but needs lots of water until it becomes established.

Fennel does not transplant well due to its deep tap root.

Notes

Use and Storage

Snip off fronds as needed. Fennel goes well with fish - place a few fresh stalks next to the fish while it is cooking.

Fresh fronds can be added to salads or soup, or use it as a garnish.

To collect the seeds, allow the plants to flower. When the flowers have turned brown, cut the stalks and place in a paper bag upside down. Hang upside down by the stems in a cool area inside. Collect the seeds as they drop out, then rinse and dry them thoroughly before storing in an airtight container.

Seeds can be used to make sausages or in other savory dishes. They work well as a pizza topping when paired with goat cheese, thinly sliced prosciutto, fresh fig and spicy arugula.

Freeze foliage for use in soups and stews or air dry and store it in an airtight container.

Profile Sheet

Name	V	H
Lavender		✓

About

This is a beautiful culinary herb that is popular for its delicate purple blooms and soothing fragrance.

Lavender also has a delicious flavor.

Like basil, oregano, and thyme, lavender is a member of the mint family.

English lavender is the most popular of all the available cultivars and is also the variety most used in cooking.

Advice for Growing

Lavender grows best in a sunny location with very well-drained soil. Ideal growing conditions for lavender are hot and dry.

Use and Storage

Too much lavender flavour can be overbearing. When cooking with it, start with small amounts and slowly add more until the desired result is achieved.

Be aware that a lot of commercially available lavender is not safe to be consumed so ensure you are growing / purchasing 'culinary grade'.

Harvest small amounts of lavender when the plant is 2 years old. A much larger harvest can be expected from the third year. Use garden sheers or a curved blade to cut through the tough stems.

Enjoy lavender in both sweet and savory dishes. Use fresh lavender in salads or homemade ice cream. It can also be used in place of rosemary in breads and marinades.

Strip the leaves off of dried stems and use them as kabobs for grilled shrimp or fruit.

Notes

Profile Sheet

Name	V	H
Mint		✓

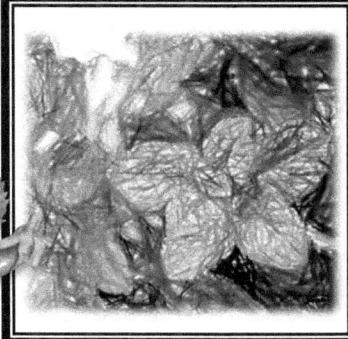

About

Mint is a nearly foolproof culinary herb. This versatile and tough plant is a good herb to start with for beginners and those with a black thumb.

Mint belongs to same plant family as many other popular herbs, including basil, oregano, and rosemary.

Peppermint and spearmint are the most popular of the many mint varieties available.

Advice for Growing

Mint prefers full sun and a more moist soil than most. If you keep the soil around your mint damp, it will produce more strongly scented leaves.

It is a very good companion plant because its strong scent repels ants and many other garden pests. It is an aggressive grower that can also become an invasive nuisance.

Plant mint in containers or sink large bottomless plastic containers into the ground to prevent mint from taking over the garden.

Notes

Use and Storage

Take clippings as needed from the plants. Look for the newest growth because it is the most flavorful. Rinse leaves thoroughly and pat dry before using.

There are many ways to use mint. It is used in ice tea and other beverages, as well as forming a key ingredient in several classic cocktails: mint juleps, mojitos and gimlets. Bruise, or muddle, the leaves before adding to drinks for best results.

To use mint in mixed green salads, roll the leaves and slice into thin sections.

Add finely chopped mint leaves to chocolate chip cookie dough before baking, or use fresh mint leaves to enhance homemade sorbet or ice cream recipes.

Excess mint can be frozen alone or in ice cube trays. It can also be dried and stored in an airtight container.

Profile Sheet

Name	V	H
Oregano		✓

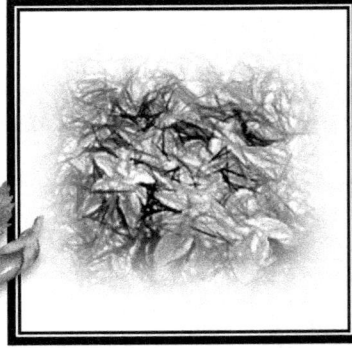

About

Oregano is very popular in Greek, Italian and Mexican cuisine. Mexican oregano is stronger than the Greek and Italian varieties, and does not work well as a substitute for the other types.

Some types of oregano work better as ornamental herbs, for example 'Kent Beauty'. This variety is grown primarily for its hop-like flowers and eye-catching foliage.

Advice for Growing

Greek and Italian oregano belong to the mint family, along with basil, rosemary, thyme and many other popular culinary herbs. These perennial varieties prefer full sun, with some afternoon shade in hot climates. Plants will perform best in well-drained soil.

n warm climates, Oregano is evergreen. In colder areas, the plants will need some protection in the form of mulch or cold frames to survive the winter. Oregano grown in portable containers can be brought indoors for fresh flavor all year long.

Notes

Use and Storage

Oregano goes very well with tomato based (Italian) dishes.

There are many other ways to use fresh oregano: in baked breads or herb butter; sprinkled over mixed salad greens; or added to homemade vinaigrettes or marinades. To release more flavour, crush the leaves with your fingers.

Add fresh oregano in the last 5 to 10 minutes of cooking as it does not do well with heat. Use dried oregano in tomato sauces, soups or stews that require longer cooking times.

When using dried oregano, adjust the required amount, as it is stronger when dried.

Oregano can be frozen alone or in ice cube trays with water or olive oil. It can also be dried and stored in an airtight container or preserved in butter.

Profile Sheet

Name	V	H
Parsley		✓

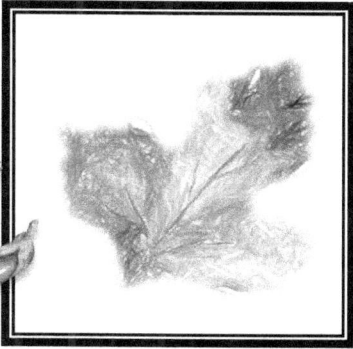

About

Parsley is easy to dismiss as an obsolete herb. However, this versatile culinary herb actually tastes good.

There are two main varieties of parsley: flat leaf (aka Italian parsley) and curled leaf. These two are mostly interchangeable, however, the flat leaf variety has a more robust flavor, while the curled variety has more tender leaves and is more often used as a garnish.

Advice for Growing

Parsley is easy to grow from seeds or nursery transplants. It likes plenty of sun, but it can also grow in partial shade.

Grow in rich, moist soil, and ensure the plants receive plenty of water.

Notes

Use and Storage

Fresh parsley is ideal for adding
color to a dinner plate. To add some bright, fresh flavor to a dish, sprinkle finely chopped fresh leaves over the food

To harvest, trim fresh sprigs as needed. Cut leafy stems from the base of the plant to encourage bushier growth.

Fresh parsley stems are perfect for making stocks, broths, soups or braises. Parsley is one of the main ingredients
in a classic "bouquet garni." To make your own, secure parsley stems, sprigs of fresh thyme and whole bay leaves with unwaxed kitchen string. Add to the pot while making soups, stews and broth. Rand discard when finished.

Parsley can be frozen and used in cooked dishes, but will no longer be viable as a garnish. Avoid drying because too much of the flavor is lost in the process.

Profile Sheet

Name	V	H
Rosemary		✓

About

Rosemary is a versatile, fragrant herb native
to the Mediterranean region. It is popular for its pungent, pine-like flavor that adds a distinctive taste to dishes ranging from grilled fish to beef roasts to wild game. Rosemary is also a visually appealing herb, Its woody stems allow it to be pruned into a conical Christmas tree-like shape and adds visual quality to your herb garden or window sill.

Advice for Growing

Rosemary is a member of the mint family, along with basil, oregano, thyme and many others. As with the other members of this herb family, it prefers a warm, sunny
spot in well-drained soil.
 Rosemary can grow into a large evergreen shrub in hot climates, but it is not hardy in colder areas. To survive, it needs to be brought inside when temperatures drop below freezing.

Notes

Use and Storage

There are many ways to use rosemary in the kitchen. To use as a marinade for meats and chicken, strip the leaves from the woody stems and crush them with your fingers to release the oils.
Combine Worcestershire sauce, olive oil, garlic and crushed rosemary to make a wonderful marinade for steaks. Stuff chicken or other poultry with whole fresh rosemary sprigs, lemon wedges and cloves of garlic. Finely chopped leaves are a delicious addition to soups, stews and salad dressings.
To harvest, clip fresh sprigs as needed. Rosemary will keep in the refrigerator for approx. one week
For larger harvests, rosemary can be frozen alone or in ice cube trays with water or oil. It can also be dried or preserved in olive oil or vinegar, or finely chop the leaves to make herb butter or seasoned salt mix.

Profile Sheet

Name	V	H
Sage		✓

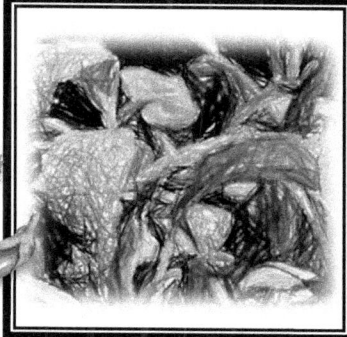

About

Sage is known as a culinary herb and medicinal plant. Native to the Mediterranean region, it was used by Ancient Romans for its healing qualities. Later, the French grew large amounts of sage for tea.

Today, sage is considered a classic ingredient in holiday stuffing and other rich dishes.

Sage is a member of the mint family, along with basil, oregano, thyme, rosemary and many others.

Advice for Growing

Sage is an attractive perennial in USDA zones 5 to 8 and does not do well in extreme heat or cold. It prefers full sun and light, well-drained soil. Loose soil, raised garden beds or containers are ideal for growing sage.

Do not plant sage too close to cucumbers as its strong flavor can have an adverse affect on the fruit.

Notes

Use and Storage

Sage is best known for its use in holiday stuffing recipes. It pairs beautifully with foods high in fat and oil, and is often used to make sausage and other meats for this reason. It is also perfect with buttery pasta dishes. For a quick and easy meal, sauté fresh sage leaves in butter and toss with penne pasta, sliced grilled sausage and some freshly grated Parmigiano-Reggiano cheese. Fresh sage sautéed in a browned butter sauce goes well with butternut squash ravioli.

Best enjoyed fresh, however sage can also be dried or frozen, either alone or in ice cube trays with water or oil. Fresh sage can be preserved in butter. Dried leaves can be used to infuse vinegar and honey, or used to make an herbed salt that is then used for meat rubs.

NOTE: Check with your medical practitioner before using Chamomile for medicinal purposes.

Profile Sheet

Name	V	H
Stevia		✓

About

Stevia has been used for centuries in South America as a natural sweetener. Its popularity has grown in other parts of the world because it offers a calorie-free alternative to regular processed sugar and other sweeteners.

Advice for Growing

As a native to tropical regions, stevia is an annual that enjoys most climates. It grows best in warm, humid weather, but needs good air circulation to stay healthy. Grow in a sunny spot with a little afternoon shade
in warmer areas.

Root rot is an issue for many culinary herbs, including stevia. Be sure to provide loose, well-drained soil. Raised beds and containers work best if you have dense clay or other soil that does not drain well.

Notes

Use and Storage

Stevia is up to 15 times stronger than regular cane sugar, but the amount of sweetness varies depending on growing conditions and when the leaves are harvested. Start by adding very small amounts to your drinks and recipes until you find the right balance.

To harvest, clip stems or individual leaves as needed. Use leaves either fresh or dried. Dry cuttings outside, in a food dehydrator or in a low heat oven. Discard the stems once the leaves are thoroughly dried. Crumble or grind the dried leaves into a powder and store in an airtight container in a cool, dark place.

Fresh leaves are used to sweeten tea and other drinks. Powdered leaves can be used directly in recipes or to make extracts, tinctures or syrups that can be stored in a dark bottle in your refrigerator for up to one year.

Profile Sheet

Name	V	H
Thyme		✓

About

This aromatic herb is well known for its ornamental and medicinal qualities.

Thyme is popular for both its flavor and fragrance, as well as the way it grows in garden beds as a border plant, and how it spills over low walls and containers.

Thyme is a member of the mint family, along with basil, oregano, rosemary and lavender.

Of the many varieties of thyme available, German and lemon are the two better-known ones. German thyme is aromatic and popular for cooking, and Lemon Thyme has a lovely citrus aroma and flavour.

Advice for Growing

Thyme prefers full sun and needs well-drained soil to thrive.

Grow in soil that is slightly more alkaline than other herbs, with a pH just above 7.0. If needed, add a little lime to the soil or limestone mulch around the plants.

Notes

Use and Storage

To harvest, clip off a few stems as needed. To remove leaves, hold the stems at the top and gently pull down the length of the stem with your fingers. Discard the stems or use to make stocks and broths.

Add thyme early in the cooking process in order to release all of its flavor. Sprinkle fresh leaves into pasta sauces or add them directly into soups, stews, and braises. Tie whole thyme stems together with parsley stems and a bay leaves to create a classic "bouquet garni" to season soups and broths.

Combine fresh thyme with rosemary and sage for a marinade for grilled meat. Before roasting, lightly toss potatoes, carrots or other root vegetables in a little olive oil, fresh thyme and some salt and pepper. Thyme can also be dried, frozen alone or in ice cubes with water or oil, or preserved in olive oil or butter.

Profile Sheet

Name	V	H

About

Advice for Growing

Notes

Use and Storage

Profile Sheet

Name	V	H

About

Advice for Growing

Notes

Use and Storage

Profile Sheet

Name	V	H

About

Advice for Growing

Notes

Use and Storage

Profile Sheet

Name	V	H

About

Advice for Growing

Notes

Use and Storage

Profile Sheet

Name	V	H

About

Advice for Growing

Notes

Use and Storage

Profile Sheet

Name	V	H

About

Advice for Growing

Notes

Use and Storage

Profile Sheet

Name	V	H

About

Advice for Growing

Notes

Use and Storage

Profile Sheet

Name	V	H

About

Advice for Growing

Notes

Use and Storage

Profile Sheet

Name	V	H

About

Advice for Growing

Notes

Use and Storage

Profile Sheet

Name	V	H

About

Advice for Growing

Notes

Use and Storage

Profile Sheet

Name	V	H

About

Advice for Growing

Notes

Use and Storage

Profile Sheet

Name	V	H

About

Advice for Growing

Notes

Use and Storage

Profile Sheet

Name	V	H

About

Advice for Growing

Notes

Use and Storage

Profile Sheet

Name	V	H

About

Advice for Growing

Notes

Use and Storage

Profile Sheet

Name	V	H

About

Advice for Growing

Notes

Use and Storage

Profile Sheet

Name	V	H

About

Advice for Growing

Notes

Use and Storage

Profile Sheet

Name	V	H

About

Advice for Growing

Notes

Use and Storage

Profile Sheet

Name	V	H

About

Advice for Growing

Notes

Use and Storage

Profile Sheet

Name	V	H

About

Advice for Growing

Notes

Use and Storage

Profile Sheet

Name	V	H

About

Advice for Growing

Notes

Use and Storage

Profile Sheet

Name	V	H

About

Advice for Growing

Notes

Use and Storage

Profile Sheet

Name	V	H

About

Advice for Growing

Notes

Use and Storage

Profile Sheet

Name	V	H

About

Advice for Growing

Notes

Use and Storage

Profile Sheet

Name	V	H

About

Advice for Growing

Notes

Use and Storage

Profile Sheet

Name	V	H

About

Advice for Growing

Notes

Use and Storage

Profile Sheet

Name	V	H

About

Advice for Growing

Notes

Use and Storage

Profile Sheet

Name	V	H

About

Advice for Growing

Notes

Use and Storage

Profile Sheet

Name	V	H

About

Advice for Growing

Notes

Use and Storage

Profile Sheet

Name	V	H

About

Advice for Growing

Notes

Use and Storage

Profile Sheet

Name	V	H

About

Advice for Growing

Notes

Use and Storage

Recipe

For

PREP TIME

COOKING TIME

SERVINGS

CALORIES/ SERVING

RATING

Ingredients

Method

Notes

Recipe

For

PREP TIME

COOKING TIME

CALORIES/ SERVING

SERVINGS

RATING

Ingredients

Method

Notes

PREP TIME

COOKING TIME

CALORIES/ SERVING

SERVINGS

RATING

Recipe

For

Ingredients

Method

Notes

Recipe

For

PREP TIME

COOKING TIME

CALORIES/ SERVING

SERVINGS

RATING

Ingredients

Method

Notes

Recipe

For

PREP TIME

COOKING TIME

CALORIES/ SERVING

SERVINGS

RATING

Ingredients

Method

Notes

Recipe

For

PREP TIME

COOKING TIME

SERVINGS

CALORIES/ SERVING

RATING

Ingredients

Method

Notes

PREP TIME

COOKING TIME

SERVINGS

CALORIES/ SERVING

RATING

Recipe

For

Ingredients

Method

Notes

Recipe

For

PREP TIME

COOKING TIME

SERVINGS

CALORIES/ SERVING

RATING

Ingredients

Method

Notes

Recipe

For

PREP TIME

COOKING TIME

SERVINGS

CALORIES/ SERVING

RATING

Ingredients

Method

Notes

PREP TIME	
COOKING TIME	
SERVINGS	
CALORIES/ SERVING	
RATING	

Recipe

For

Ingredients

Method

Notes

Recipe

For

PREP TIME

COOKING TIME

SERVINGS

CALORIES/ SERVING

RATING

Ingredients

Method

Notes

PREP TIME

COOKING TIME

SERVINGS

CALORIES/ SERVING

RATING

Recipe

For

Ingredients

Method

Notes

PREP TIME

COOKING TIME

SERVINGS

CALORIES/ SERVING

RATING

Recipe

For

Ingredients

Method

Notes

Recipe

For

PREP TIME

COOKING TIME

SERVINGS

CALORIES/SERVING

RATING

Ingredients

Method

Notes

Recipe

PREP TIME

COOKING TIME

SERVINGS

CALORIES/ SERVING

RATING

For

Ingredients

Method

Notes

PREP TIME	
COOKING TIME	
CALORIES/ SERVING	
SERVINGS	
RATING	

Recipe

For

Ingredients

Method

Notes

Recipe

For

PREP TIME

COOKING TIME

SERVINGS

CALORIES/ SERVING

RATING

Ingredients

Method

Notes

PREP TIME	
COOKING TIME	
CALORIES/ SERVING	
SERVINGS	
RATING	

Recipe

For

Ingredients

Method

Notes

Recipe

For

PREP TIME

COOKING TIME

SERVINGS

CALORIES/SERVING

RATING

Ingredients

Method

Notes

PREP TIME	
COOKING TIME	
SERVINGS	
CALORIES/SERVING	
RATING	

Recipe

For

Ingredients

Method

Notes

Recipe

For

PREP TIME

COOKING TIME

SERVINGS

CALORIES/SERVING

RATING

Ingredients

Method

Notes

PREP TIME	
COOKING TIME	
SERVINGS	
CALORIES/ SERVING	
RATING	

Recipe

For

Ingredients

Method

Notes

PREP TIME

COOKING TIME

SERVINGS

CALORIES/ SERVING

RATING

Recipe

For

Ingredients

Method

Notes

Recipe

For

PREP TIME

COOKING TIME

CALORIES/ SERVING

SERVINGS

RATING

Ingredients

Method

Notes

Recipe

For:

PREP TIME:

COOKING TIME:

SERVINGS:

CALORIES/ SERVING:

RATING:

Ingredients

Method

Notes

Recipe

For

PREP TIME

COOKING TIME

CALORIES/ SERVING

SERVINGS

RATING

Ingredients

Method

Notes

Recipe

For

PREP TIME

COOKING TIME

SERVINGS

CALORIES/ SERVING

RATING

Ingredients

Method

Notes

Recipe

For

- PREP TIME
- COOKING TIME
- SERVINGS
- CALORIES/SERVING
- RATING

Ingredients

Method

Notes

PREP TIME

COOKING TIME

CALORIES/ SERVING

SERVINGS

RATING

Recipe

For

Ingredients

Method

Notes

PREP TIME	

COOKING TIME	

CALORIES/ SERVING	

SERVINGS	

RATING	

Recipe

For

Ingredients

Method

Notes

Notes

Date

Date

Date

Notes

Notes

Notes

Notes

Notes

Notes

Notes

Notes

Notes

Notes

Notes

Notes

Notes

Notes

Notes

Notes

Notes

Notes

Notes

Notes

Notes

Notes

Notes

Notes

Notes

Get Your Free Credit Card Knive

"VALUED AT $17.95 IT'S NOW YOURS FOR FREE!"

Suitable for:
Vegetable
Gardening,
Outdoors,
Survival,
Camping,
Sailing,
Diving,

We're giving away these super handy Credit Card Knives for FREE! This offer will not last forever though so make sure you claim yours right now before our stock runs out!

CLAIM YOURS NOW:
harperstribune.com/knive

www.ingramcontent.com/pod-product-compliance
Lightning Source LLC
LaVergne TN
LVHW012033070526
838202LV00056B/5482